IMAGES
of America

WAWA

Wawa's prototype store in Chadds Ford, Pennsylvania, combines high-quality presentation of food and gas with easy access. These stores represent the company's flight plan for the future. (Joe Mullan photograph.)

IMAGES
of America

WAWA

Maria M. Thompson and Donald H. Price
Foreword by Richard D. Wood Jr.

ARCADIA
PUBLISHING

ISBN 978-0-7385-3631-6

Published by Arcadia Publishing
Charleston, South Carolina

Printed in the Unites States of America

Library of Congress Catalog Card Number: 2004105914

For all general information contact Arcadia Publishing at:
Telephone 843-853-2070
Fax 843-853-0044
E-mail sales@arcadiapublishing.com
For customer service and orders:
Toll-Free 1-888-313-2665

Visit us on the Internet at www.arcadiapublishing.com

In 1980, president Richard D. Wood Jr. and chairman Grahame Wood pose outside Wawa's main office, an old Wood family house called Red Roof. (Robert McManus photograph.)

CONTENTS

ACKNOWLEDGMENTS

Writing may be a solitary task, but this book project was collaborative from the beginning. The story of today's company, told by my coauthor Don Price, comes to life through his powerful photographs of people, places, and events at Wawa taken since he arrived on the scene in 1979. Thanks are due his assistant Carolyn Bratton, who assembled and formatted his text.

For images of both the distant past and more recent era, I relied on the Wawa Collection at the Hagley Museum and Library, where Jon M. Williams, the Andrew W. Mellon curator of prints and photographs, was always accommodating and helpful. I am grateful to Jon and to photographer Martin W. Kane, whose brilliant photographs of Wawa appeared in a 1992 exhibit at Hagley entitled "Works." I also thank the Brandywine River Museum, Free Library of Philadelphia, Historical Society of Pennsylvania, and Library Company of Philadelphia for permission to reproduce images in their collections. Other repositories, organizations, and individuals are acknowledged in captions accompanying their work.

Two gentlemen in Millville deserve special mention. Robert Francois, president of the Millville Historical Society, and Dale Wettstein of Steelman Photographics are to be commended for their preservation of historic materials. In addition, their affection for and knowledge of Millville and its manufacturing heritage help infuse photographs and clippings with meaning.

The late Edward F. R. Wood Jr. spent years assembling a documented Wood family genealogy and collecting historic photographs to illustrate a proposed book. He died before completing the task, but this book is richer because of his work.

Without the help of Tom Laudenslager, a retired Wawa vice president, I could not have written captions about milk processing or dairy equipment. I thank him, as I do members of Wawa's public relations department, upon whose shoulders this book stands. Christine McCarthy organized hundreds of photographs, slides, and audiovisual materials, in addition to newsletters and in-house bulletins. Mandy Lain, associate relations coordinator, kept the ship afloat by cheerfully answering questions, retrieving and duplicating materials, and providing a carbohydrate snack at just the right moment. Karen Owsley helped select the images and then worked her magic with the scanner. She was responsible for digital imaging and layout—so, what you see is what she did.

None of this would have happened without Lori Bruce, Wawa's manager of communications and public relations. She established the framework within which we worked and had a guiding hand in all phases of the project, from choosing themes and images to layout and editing.

FOREWORD

Wawa has a long and rich history dating back to 1803, transitioning from an iron foundry to textile mills, then to dairy processing, and currently convenience store retailing. The company was incorporated in 1865 by my great-great-grandfather, Richard Davis Wood.

While each business cycle had its moments, the most important date in our company's history was April 16, 1964, the date of opening the first Wawa Food Market in Folsom, Pennsylvania. During the early 1960s, the textile business was in the final stages of being liquidated, and home delivery of milk, on which the Wawa Dairy's business was dependent, was in a decline as the channel of distribution for milk changed to purchases at supermarkets.

To give perspective, the dairy's profit in 1963 had declined from $54,000 in 1962 to $31,000 in 1963. Fast-forward 40 years to 2003, and this latter amount was earned in six hours. The modern-day hero was my cousin, Grahame Wood. Having participated in the demise of the textile business and witnessing the deterioration of the dairy, he stepped into the breach and opened a small store to sell milk. The new business was profitable immediately.

As the number of stores grew, the volume of milk sold through them almost exactly offset the decline in home delivery. Finally, in 1976, the dairy exited the home delivery business. But this was only the beginning for a retailer that today averages over 1.3 million customer transactions each day in five states.

What has driven this extraordinary growth? Certainly the societal trend of two wage earners in a household and the resulting time-starved consumer has been a driver of convenience. Other trends include obsolescence of both the mom-and-pop grocery store and the corner gas station; the move to grazing from formal family meals; technological advances speeding customer through-put; and the consumer demand for immediate consumption—I'm hungry, I'm thirsty, I'm out of gas, I'm out of cigarettes. The wind has been at our back with respect to societal trends. But the overwhelming driver of growth at Wawa has been the people who work here, the values they live by, and the commitment they bring to their jobs everyday.

Management can sit in a windowless room and devise the world's greatest strategies, but if the people in an organization are not aligned, this goes for naught. The people who work at Wawa are a special breed. Their commitment is not just to a job. It is to each other, their customers, and the communities they serve. When someone falls ill, an incredible support network is immediately and voluntarily formed for that person and his family. Stores employ people with disabilities because there is the right job for each person, whether it is stocking the cold box or being a coffee host or hostess. In return, the store gets a dedicated, loyal employee whom the customers enjoy and fellow store members respect. This is a win for the disabled individual, the store team, and customers. Wawa associates participate in and raise money for a myriad of community and charitable causes. They are passionate about reaching out to give a hand up to others who are less fortunate. Equally so, they are passionate about their customers, for example, keeping stores open through blizzards and hurricanes, remembering customers' names and even their birthdays, and often helping customers in times of crisis. We strive to be the "Cheers" of convenience stores, simplifying our customers' lives by offering them a moment of peace in their stressful day.

The core values of Wawa are to value people, delight the customer, embrace change, do the right thing, do things right, and have a passion for winning. These values have driven the company's growth. If these values were not practiced, there would be a lack of alignment around strategies. Our business platform is the traditional three-legged stool: people, facilities, and the offer. The strategies are recruiting and retaining the best people, finding and developing world-class facilities, and providing customers an overpowering offer.

This book illustrates how our business has adapted over time. More importantly, it is a celebration of people—people who have driven this adaptation through time, people who have advanced the company's growth, and people who will continue to enable future growth. I am proud and humbled to be included among those people.

—Richard D. Wood Jr.
Chairman and CEO

One

ENTERPRISING QUAKERS

English Quaker Richard Wood arrived in Philadelphia with his family before 1683, when he served on the grand jury. Like many others, he came to Pennsylvania to escape political turmoil and religious persecution. William Penn established a colony where government, laws, and social context were based on Quaker ideals of tolerance and harmony. Many legends grew out of Penn's beliefs and practices. One of the best known is a 1682 Friendship Treaty with the Lenni Lenape that appeared as an engraved illustration in a 19th-century Wood family history.

RICHARD WOOD,
BORN IN PHILAD-A. 11 Mo. 1694,
DIED IN GREENWICH, 8 Mo. 3, 1759,
WAS BURIED IN THIS LOT;
ENCLOSED IN THE SPRING OF 1868
BY HIS GREAT GRANDSON
DR. GEO. B. WOOD OF PHILAD-A.
HIS GREAT-GREAT-GRANDSON GEO. W. SHEPPARD
WITH HIS WIFE RUTH, AND SON JOHN,
RESIDING ON THE FARM.

When Richard Wood crossed the Delaware River from Pennsylvania to New Jersey, he represented the third generation of his family in British America. Quakers established Salem in West Jersey in 1675, and Wood settled nearby before 1716. Later he moved to Stow Creek near Greenwich and served as justice of pleas and peace from 1739 to 1747. A marble tablet honoring him is part of a wall surrounding a family cemetery.

Richard Wood and Ebenezer Miller Jr. developed the 100-acre Union Mill site between 1745–1749, when they sold it for $15 an acre (a high price) to Thomas and Richard Penn. The property changed hands several times before David Cooper Wood and James Smith purchased it in the early 19th century. The Union House, built for the miller c. 1728 and extensively modified, was restored in the 1970s.

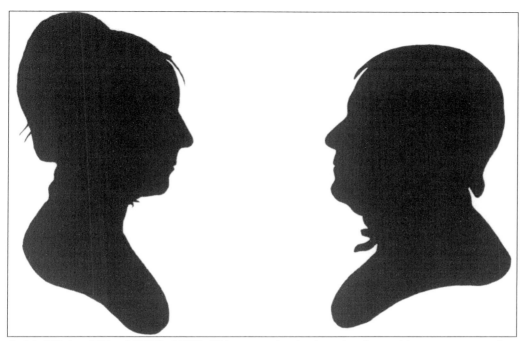

A third Richard Wood (1755–1822), fifth generation in America, began his career as a teacher but gravitated toward the mercantile pursuits of his father and grandfather. This proved a lucrative choice, and he built a store on Greenwich's main street that he operated by himself or in association with members of his extended family. In 1780, he married Ann Cooper of Gloucester County, but she died in 1783, leaving him with an infant son David Cooper Wood. Ten years later, he married Elizabeth Bacon (above) and in 1795 built the brick house (below) in which they reared nine children. The house and Wood's store are part of the Greenwich Historic District on the National Register of Historic Places. Two of Richard Wood's sons, David and Richard, had leading roles in the business enterprises that spawned Wawa.

In December 1980, some members of the Wood family gathered in front of the Wood store to celebrate a restoration overseen by Mrs. Richard D. Wood (top row, fourth from left). The frame building is a rare surviving 18th-century building type. Recorded by the Historic American Buildings Survey in 1936, the store is on the National Register of Historic Places as part of the Greenwich Historic District. When Wood built the store, Greenwich was a thriving commercial center whose merchants imported whale oil, codfish, rum, wine, sugar, molasses, and such amenities as furniture and crystal. South Jersey's navigable waterways and protected harbors encouraged intercity commerce with exports from the fields and forests of the region being shipped to Delaware, Pennsylvania, New York, and the West Indies. Greenwich's main street, part of the King's Highway, offered access to the interior for imported goods and served as a route for farmers to bring their products to market. In the 1970s, some thought Wood's store was the oldest store in continuous existence in the country. If so, it was the first Wawa.

Two

MERCHANTS AND
MANUFACTURERS

A century before Wawa Dairy Farms delivered milk, Wood family foundries and mills in Millville, New Jersey, on the Maurice River, produced manufactured goods ranging from cast-iron stove plates and iron pipes to umbrella cloth, towels, and diapers. Sloops and schooners laden with iron products or cotton goods went to ports all along the East Coast. When the railroad came, goods also went overland to major distribution points. Almost from the beginning, Wood family offices in Philadelphia handled sales. (Courtesy Steelman Photographics.)

David Cooper Wood (1781–1859), oldest son of Richard Wood, was a merchant and entrepreneur whose career began in his father's store in Greenwich and grew to include stores in Port Elizabeth, Woodbury, and Dividing Creek. He owned or had interest in farms and ore lands in Delaware that supplemented his vast holdings in New Jersey. His earliest iron venture was Cumberland Furnace on the Manumuskin Creek. From there he moved to Millville, where he and others established a furnace and foundry to manufacture stove plates and iron pipe. Wood's Mansion House (below), the oldest surviving house in urban Millville, features porch supports and a fence made of Jersey bog iron cast at Millville Furnace. Once home to resident managers of the Millville Manufacturing Company, the Wood family textile business, the Mansion House now houses regional offices of Wawa.

CHEAP STORE.

THE subscriber respectfully informs his friends and the public in general, that he has just opened at the store lately occupied by Henry Rulon, in Woodbury, a neat and general assortment of new, plain and fashionable

DRY-GOODS,

Suitable for the approaching season :

ALSO, A GENERAL ASSORTMENT OF

Groceries, Ironmongery,

Queens-ware, Earthen-ware, Paints, Oils, &c. &c.

Together with a variety of articles in the

APOTHECARY LINE;

All of which he will dispose of on the most reasonable terms for cash, or various kinds of country produce.

Tavern keepers who are desirous of keeping an assortment of good liquors, are requested to call and examine those of the subscriber, and if disposed to favor him with their custom, they may depend upon being furnished with those of the best quality, at the most moderate prices.

DAVID C. WOOD.

Woodbury, May 1, 1808.

Price is always important, and when David C. Wood took over Henry Rulon's store in Woodbury, he put into practice lessons learned at Wood and Bacon's store in Greenwich. In addition, Wood had experience in shipping. As part owner of sloops and shallops, the latter a boat powered by oars and sails used in shallow, tidal waters, he sent products like cheese, pork, lard, and flour across the Delaware Bay and around Cape May to ports in such faraway places as Cuba. Perhaps this is where he got "Spanish segars" that cost $15 per 1,000. The 1808 advertisement for "Dry-Goods suitable for the approaching season" attests to the wealth and variety of goods offered in general stores in outlying regions. Woodbury is near Camden across the river from Philadelphia, which at that time was the largest city in North America, and this proximity is reflected in the relative sophistication of Wood's comprehensive offering. In early 1813, Wood left Woodbury to put his considerable energy into Millville Furnace, a venture his father judged a very expensive concern.

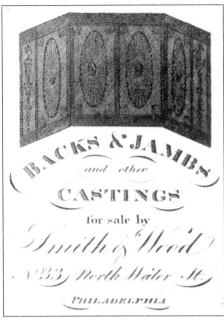

In the early years of the 19th century, David Wood seemed to be everywhere in the Philadelphia–South Jersey region. He was able to appear omnipresent because he had an extensive network of partnerships and cooperative ventures. The most enduring was that of Smith and Wood. They established the furnace at Millville and sold their iron castings from Philadelphia, starting a marketing practice followed by subsequent Wood family enterprises.

Watering commissions in Philadelphia and other cities were charged with providing potable water to city residents and businesses. Construction of Philadelphia's new waterworks at Fairmount on the Schuylkill River began in 1812, and it opened in 1815. The second phase of construction, from 1819 to 1822, used pipe from Millville Furnace. Considered an engineering marvel, the waterworks attracted tourists such as English writer Charles Dickens. (Courtesy Library Company of Philadelphia.)

Richard Davis Wood was born in Greenwich in 1799 and, like his half-brother David, worked in his father's store. He broadened this early experience by working for an uncle who was also a merchant, and in 1820 with a Bacon cousin as partner, he moved to Salem to open his own store. Wood went to Philadelphia for merchandise, and to save money he arranged cheap transport, but the vessel leaked, destroying the perishables and damaging the rest of the shipment. He salvaged the venture by selling damaged goods at bargain prices, and buyers flocked to his shop. After two years in Salem, he was ready for Philadelphia, where he and partner William L. Abbott introduced a system of selling goods for cash at 5 percent advance. R. D. Wood married Julianna Randolph in 1832, and this silhouette of the family was made in Edouard's studio in 1843.

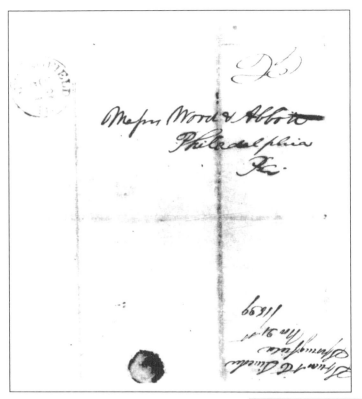

Richard D. Wood and William L. Abbott owned a store on Market Street in Philadelphia, where they sold imported woolen blankets, bobbins, tapes, yard goods, hemp, and lead. By the mid-1830s, they had many customers along the upper Mississippi River, in states like Missouri and Illinois, that Wood called "the western business." Pursuing delinquent accounts was an unpleasant and time-consuming task. In 1838, Wood and Abbott hired solicitors in Springfield, Illinois, to represent them in claims against several customers. Abraham Lincoln passed the bar in 1836 and moved to Springfield the following year. He and John Todd Stuart advertised as "attorneys and counsellors at law." There are three known letters signed by A. Lincoln to Wood and Abbott. The one shown above is from 1839.

In the 1840s, R. D. Wood entertained the idea of establishing a bank. As a merchant, he was in the money business when he discounted advances on customers' orders and issued notes. As a businessman, he enjoyed a close association with the city's bankers whom he supported through the depressions and bank wars of the 1830s. Wood served as director of the Philadelphia Bank in 1835 and 1837–1864. In 1837, the Philadelphia Bank occupied a new building, designed by William Strickland (above), on the southwest corner of Fourth and Chestnut Streets, where in the 1850s Wood established an office. Later the bank moved out, and in May 1859 he bought 400 Chestnut Street for $76,500. After his death, his sons demolished the building and in 1880 retained Quaker architect Addison Hutton to design the high-rise R. D. Wood building. (Courtesy Historical Society of Pennsylvania.)

R. D. WOOD BUILDING, FOURTH AND CHESTNUT STREETS.

By the early 1840s, the glory days of canal transportation were over, and Philadelphia entered the race to find alternate routes to western markets. R. D. Wood and six other businessmen met in 1845 to consider "a continuous railway to connect Philadelphia with the great West." The committee of seven presided over town meetings held at Philadelphia's Chinese Museum in 1846. (Courtesy Print and Picture Collection, Free Library of Philadelphia.)

As an organizer and director of the Pennsylvania Railroad, which opened a through route to Pittsburgh in 1854, Wood understood the need for a rolling mill to produce iron rails. Investors wanted to expand the Cambria Furnace at Johnstown, and construction began on an ironworks in 1853. Money ran out. R. D. Wood formed Wood, Morrell & Company to lease the property and complete the project. (Courtesy Historical Society of Pennsylvania.)

Just as Wood judged the Pennsylvania Railroad the making of Philadelphia, he knew the introduction of rail lines into southern New Jersey would dramatically affect the economy. In 1853, he helped organize the West Jersey Railroad, with routes to Woodbury, Glassboro, and Bridgeton and later promoted a line between Millville and Glassboro that was chartered in 1859. Years before, he noted the rising popularity of Cape May as a "watering place," and by 1863 summer visitors could go there by train. That year, Wood built a house on the ocean, named Sea Brink, in honor of his 31st wedding anniversary. By the time of the nation's centennial in 1876, Cape May was one of the country's most prominent seasonal resorts. (Courtesy Hagley Museum and Library.)

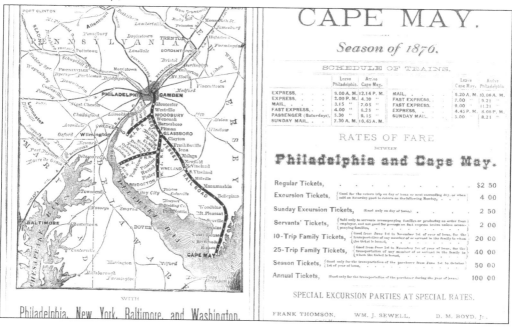

When David C. Wood operated Millville Furnace, he produced a small amount of decorative ironwork but relied upon more utilitarian products like stove plates and pipes to sustain the industrial venture, not always successfully. A combination of factors led to worrisome times in the 1840s, when David sought the advice of his brother Richard, who began managing the furnace and bought the bankrupt property in 1850. Two years later, R. D. Wood received an order for iron railing around Penn Square, seen above in an 1854 photograph. Afterwards, the ironworks combined decorative and utilitarian styles in a complete line of lampposts suitable for urban streetscapes. (Above, courtesy Library Company of Philadelphia; below, courtesy Hagley Museum and Library.)

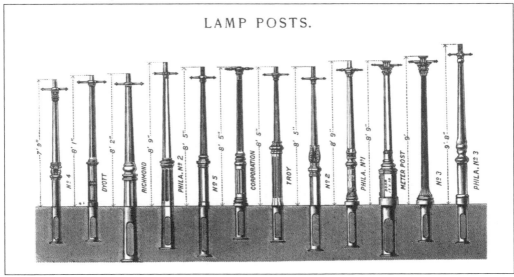

After R. D. Wood assumed control of Millville Furnace and built a new foundry in 1851, he devoted attention to production of pig iron and finished products like pipe and lampposts. Eventually, R. D. Wood & Company expanded to include ironworks in Camden and Florence, New Jersey, that specialized in large-scale industrial fixtures like turbines and gas machinery in addition to plain and metered lampposts. Mathews' fire hydrants, stamped R. D. Wood & Company, are still in use in New Orleans, Charlottesville, and Madison, Wisconsin. When R. D. Wood died in 1869, management of the iron business passed to his sons Richard, Edward, Walter, and Stuart, with son George overseeing cotton manufacturing. The brothers served on one another's boards, so in effect, family management continued. Offices for all businesses were maintained in the R. D. Wood building at 400 Chestnut Street. (Right, courtesy Hagley Museum and Library.)

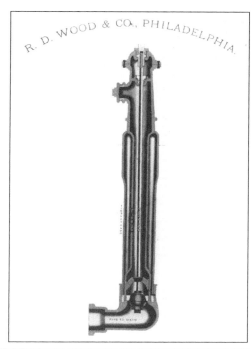

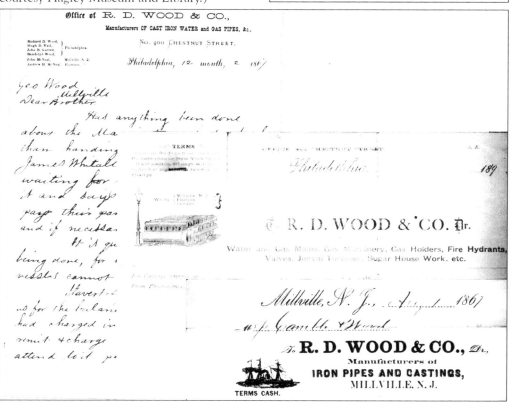

23

Located 25 miles from the mouth of the Maurice River at Delaware Bay, Millville developed from an earlier settlement called Shingle Landing, a fitting name that described one local resource, cedar shingles, shipped to Philadelphia and other cities. The surrounding oak and pine forests yielded cordwood and lumber while the light sandy soil and rich mineral deposits fostered growth of a glass industry. The King's Highway crossed the Maurice River near the sawmills at the Union Mill, and this combination of overland route and waterway led David Wood and James Smith to dam the river and dig a small canal to furnish horsepower for their iron furnace. Seen here in the 1820s, the site changed dramatically in the 1850s, when R. D. Wood purchased the property, dug a larger canal, expanded the foundry, and constructed a cotton mill. At Millville, Wood's vision of a manufacturing complex relied on use of an existing resource, water power, in a new way and development of an unrelated industry, cotton manufacturing, to combat dwindling supplies of bog iron while still offering products directly from the manufacturer.

The developed Millville site contained, in addition to the furnace and foundry, a cotton mill, glassworks, grist- and sawmills, and a gasworks. Called New Jersey Mills at Millville, the complex expanded in 1862 with construction of the Manantico Bleach and Dye Works. Later, the mill, sewing, and weaving rooms, the bleachery, and storehouses were collectively known as Millville Manufacturing Company. (Courtesy Steelman Photographics.)

During the Civil War, R. D. Wood built a bleachery at Millville to expand the type and quality of cotton goods available for sale. Fabric off the loom is known to the industry as gray goods because of its color and must be bleached before it can be dyed. Removing cotton's natural waxes and the sizing agents added to yarns during weaving requires several bleaching processes. (Courtesy Hagley Museum and Library.)

All six of R. D. Wood's sons joined him in business, but it was George (1842–1926) who took to textile manufacturing, traveling to England in 1866 to purchase equipment and hire skilled operators for the newly incorporated Millville Manufacturing Company. Because of increased demand, father and son built another bleachery at Millville in 1868 and added storehouses and a company store. They built a smaller version of the Millville cotton mill at Mays Landing in Atlantic County to produce towels and washcloths, which it did until operations ceased in 1949. While in the midst of expansion in 1868, Wood sought authorization from the state legislature to dam the Maurice River at Millville and create a pond three and a half miles long, covering 1,100 acres with a 24-foot fall. R. D. Wood considered the dam his greatest achievement. He died on April 1, 1869.

Viewed from the water in 1907, the Millville Manufacturing Company was a vast complex of buildings housing a wide range of industrial activity. Manantico Bleach and Dye Works employed 250 workers in 1906 and nearly doubled that number 10 years later because of increased demand for domestic textiles during World War I. Through the 1950s, fabric woven and dyed at Millville was made into flags. (Courtesy Hagley Museum and Library.)

The cotton mill employed over 500 workers who produced high-quality yarns and cloths of different types. In 1912, about 54,000 yards of twills, pocketings, and towellings were made daily. These piece goods and 24 million yards of yarn required 10,800 pounds of raw cotton each day, with exports going to Cuba, Puerto Rico, the Philippines, and Turkey. (Courtesy Steelman Photographics.)

In the early days, Millville's spindles and looms clanked into action powered by water and steam, and according to an 1860 state Census of Manufactures, female workers outnumbered men. By the turn of the century, more men than women worked the looms, and men, on average, received higher weekly wages. In 1921, the average weekly pay was $18.25.

Throughout the country, Red Star was a household name that meant quality diapers and nursery products made at Millville. It was the only textile plant in New Jersey that took raw cotton, spun it into yarn, which, in turn, was woven into cloth, bleached, and finished. Seamstresses like those seen here made Red Star products. (Courtesy Steelman Photographics.)

The introduction of rayon and other synthetic fabrics eroded demand for cotton goods. Manufacturers responded to the challenge in various ways. Millville relied on the popularity of its Red Star nursery line (right) to serve a niche market and developed new finishes to make cotton stain and wrinkle resistant. Colorfast dyeing processes improved cotton's chance to remain popular as an option for dress goods. A special edition of the *Millville Manufacturing Company News* celebrated the company's 150th anniversary in 1953. On a page with photographs of the city league champion Milmaco softball team and a retirement gathering, Miss America 1953, Neva Jane Langley, is shown wearing a cotton sateen gown of Everglaze fabric made at Millville and sold through George Wood, Sons & Company. (Below, courtesy Robert Francois.)

Most comfortable for baby, cost less!
You have a wide choice in

Red ★ Star
Birdseye Diapers

THE BEST KNOWN DIAPER BRAND NAME
FOR OVER 75 YEARS
George Wood, Sons & Co.
Independence Square, Philadelphia 5, Pa.

lucky is the baby
whose mother chooses
these **RED STAR** layette items

RED STAR birdseye diapers are non-chafing, super-absorbent and extra-wearing . . . in boxes of 12.

27x27 size **3**15   30x30 size **3**65   20x40 size **3**75

hese fluffy soft diapers are gentle on baby's tender skin. Unsurpassed for durability and absorbency, they feature two selvedge edges and two emmed edges. Convenient boxes of 12.

RED STAR plastic and acetate diaper holders eliminate all pins.

boy and girl styles **98**c

A panty with a built-in diaper holder . . . adjusts to fit under the tummy, eliminates all pins, does not bind. Lace trimmed for girls; plain for boys. White, pastels. S-M-L-XL.

New mill buildings in the right foreground and the Manantico Bleachery on the left surround the 1856 cotton mill, nearly at the right center of this 1929 view. The foundry, glass- and gasworks, engine rooms, and storehouses are at the top of the photograph. After the turn of the century, the business endured, with sporadic bursts during the world wars. Increased costs of raw materials and labor drove textile manufacturing south. Introduction of rayon and other man-made fibers spelled momentary doom for cottons, and although the company bought mills in Massachusetts and Alabama, it was too little too late. Equipment liquidation began in 1958 and sale of the company followed in the 1960s. A spectacular blaze destroyed the cotton mill in November 1976. (Courtesy Hagley Museum and Library.)

Three

WAWA

The Station, Wawa, Pa.

Called Wawa by 1884, the station at the junction of the east and west branches of Chester Creek had many earlier names. First it was Pennellton, and later Baltimore Junction described its importance as a link between the Philadelphia and Baltimore Central Railroad and the West Chester and Philadelphia Railroad. In the 1870s, some folks called the place West Chester Junction, but that name died out too. Built in 1867 and enlarged in 1892, Wawa's station also housed a post office. The complex burned in 1911, and the rebuilt station met the same fate in the late 1980s. (Courtesy Keith Lockhart.)

The town of Wawa takes its name from a Native American word for the Canada goose. Among the Ojibwa, the word means "wild goose" or "land of the big goose." The Ojibwa language is part of the Algonkian language stock that also includes Lenape, which was spoken by people native to southeastern Pennsylvania. The town adjacent to Wawa on both the rail line and the Chester Creek is called Lenni after the Lenni Lenape tribes who lived and hunted locally. In the mid-19th century, many textile mills, including one at Lenni, lined this section of the creek. Lenni mill closed and Edward Worth bought land nearby, where he built a substantial stone house in a parklike setting. He called the house "Wawa" because the milldam at Lenni attracted large numbers of Canada geese. In 1906, N. C. Wyeth (1882–1945) painted *The Hunter* as part of a series called "The Indian in His Solitude" that appeared in the June 1907 issue of *The Outing Magazine*. (Collection of the Brandywine River Museum.)

George Wood (1842–1926) rented a newly built house in the Queen Anne style from Wawa landowner and developer Edward Worth. Known as Red Roof because of its Victorian decoration and colorful roof, the house was purchased in 1892 by Wood, who asked Quaker architect Addison Hutton (1834–1916) to design stables and additions to the property. The alterations served Wood and his family until 1915, when he decided to demolish the Victorian house and build a new residence in the Colonial Revival style. He selected William L. Baily and George G. Bassett for the job, asking that they leave the gardens undisturbed. The family occupied the house in April 1917, and it stayed in family hands until transferred to the company, where today it serves as part of the main office.

Russian American artist Lazar Raditz (1887–1958) painted two identical portraits of George Wood in 1915. One hangs in the board room at Red Roof and shows Wood at 73 in the attire of a country gentleman. This apparent leisure was well deserved. Wood was not only a cotton manufacturer and president of the Millville Manufacturing Company and Mays Landing Water Power Company but also head of his own firm of commission dry goods merchants, George Wood Sons & Company, with offices in Philadelphia, New York, Boston, and St. Louis. Wood acquired a love of country life and interest in agricultural pursuits while a youngster vacationing on a large farm owned by his father, and his farm activities at Wawa had roots in his boyhood experience. At Red Roof he grew potatoes, had a small orchard with apple and peach trees, kept a dairy cow and other cattle, raised sheep and chickens, and enjoyed honey from his three beehives.

Four

WAWA DAIRY FARMS

In 1900, George Wood bought three adjoining tracts of land in Delaware County, Pennsylvania. One had remnants of buildings from Rocky Run Dairy Farm, and this became the nucleus of an expanded farm operation. Wawa Dairy Farms opened in 1902 to sell milk bottled under sanitary conditions from cows certified as healthy and free from disease. People were concerned about disease transmission through milk consumption, and George Wood saw an opportunity to provide safe milk to a growing urban market. (Courtesy Hagley Museum and Library.)

Cows from the Isle of Guernsey were brought to the United States in 1840 and gained popularity after the founding of the American Guernsey Cattle Club in 1877. By 1890, they were the cow of choice for producer-distributors like George Wood because of their gentle dispositions, intermediate size, and production of high-butterfat, high-protein milk. A bull named Stars and Stripes sired these four calves.

George Wood asked Philadelphia architect Charles Hillman (1859–1934) to design a sanitary dairy or milk house where fresh milk could be cooled, bottled, and stored under the super safe conditions required to market certified milk. The dairy began operating in 1902 and continued production until 1929, when this building was modified for other use. It was demolished in 1951. (Courtesy Hagley Museum and Library.)

It is thought the word *dairy* comes from the Middle English word *dey*, which described a maidservant in charge of livestock, and that *dairy* meant the part of the farm where the dey worked. Whatever the word's origin, these dairymaids, or milkmaids, are icons from a bygone era. They are posed in front of a white clapboard building. The aprons and bonnets attest to the sanitary aspects of their work, while the pails with pouring spouts demonstrate the practicality of their twice-daily task. No record survives of additional activities they may have performed. Farms at this time had strict divisions of labor, and there was a hierarchy among workers, with field hands at the bottom and the herdsman at the top. The dairy operation had its own hierarchy, and at Wawa, by World War I, men had primary responsibility for milking. (Courtesy Hagley Museum and Library.)

Efficient transportation, on and off the farm, made all the difference in bringing a perishable product to market. Sam Johnson, shown here with field horses (above), brought supplementary feed to the cows and also helped them to the milking barn. Once milked, the cows returned to the field, but their milk required speedy processing to be ready for market. Bottles, crated at the dairy and sent by wagon to the Wawa Station, seen below c. 1906, went for transport to Philadelphia and markets beyond. George Wood had a gentleman's agreement not to compete with small dairies near his Wawa farms, and this is why, in the early years, his milk was not distributed in his own backyard. (Courtesy Hagley Museum and Library.)

Proximity to the railroad no doubt influenced Wood's decision to establish a dairy where he did. On the main route from Philadelphia to Baltimore, the dairy had a choice between overland cart and rail routes to the city. Rail links mattered when readying milk for shipment overseas or sending it to markets along the New Jersey shore. Wawa's first seasonal office was in Atlantic City, but demand mushroomed and soon offices appeared in Ocean City, Wildwood, North Wildwood, and Cape May. City directories and a collection of milk permits granting permission to sell milk in a given locality document Wawa's presence at the Jersey shore 100 years ago.

Certified milk starts with the cow, its feed, and field conditions. The most visible human interaction occurs during milking (above). Beginning c. 1903, the Pediatric Society established standards for producing milk that was free from dirt and other impurities, had a bacteria count under a particular limit, and was handled, from field to bottle, under sanitary conditions. A 1905 Wawa brochure features letters from doctors touting the merits of Wawa milk and lauding the scientific practices observed at the farms. Laboratory testing (below) determined bacteria counts, feed-yield ratios, and butterfat content, which, at that time, was a selling point and factor in determining price. (Courtesy Hagley Museum and Library.)

WAWA

CERTIFIED·

Whole Milk, absolutely pure and scientific-
ally clean.

Every bottle bears the certificate of the
Philadelphia Pediatric Society.

Ideal food for infants, invalids, convalescents and all people
who are particular.

Clover Sweet
Milk

Bottled at the Wawa Dairy
Farms, for household use, gives
economical protection against
the dangers of ordinary mixed
milk.

———————— CALL UP ————————

WAWA DAIRY FARMS

OFFICE AND LABORATORY

22-26 So. 32d St., Philadelphia, Pa.

AGENCIES: Germantown. Camden, Atlantic City, Ocean City, Wildwood, Cape
May.

This full-page advertisement from the back cover of the 1908 edition of the *Official Guide to the University of Pennsylvania* reflects the success of George Wood's venture into a specialized segment of the market milk business. Visitors were encouraged to come to the farm and would be met Monday through Friday at the train leaving Broad Street at 2:50 p.m. A 1906 publication of the Odd Fellows, a service organization, described a visit to the dairy as "quite a treat" and praised "the great modern model dairy" at Wawa with its "own ice plant, electric light plant, milking machines and all the modern equipment." Offering certified milk was all about having control of the product through every step of production, not only because the state had regulations, but also because a code of honor among producers dictated compliance with rigorous standards.

Changes to buildings on farm and dairy property between 1910 (above) and 1920 (below) reflected new requirements in milk marketing and the growing popularity of milk as a table drink for all members of the family, not just babies and invalids. At the 1911 Philadelphia Milk Show, slogans like "Take no chances with dirty milk" and "Kill that fly" reinforced the importance of healthy cows and proper milk handling. Concerns about the spread of disease, particularly tuberculosis, through contaminated milk led to increased use of pasteurization to ensure a safe product. After 1914, Philadelphia required pasteurization of milk sold within the city, unless it was certified, and George Wood established a second herd, built new stone barns, and modified the dairy, making two separate processing units so he could satisfy customers in both markets. (Courtesy Hagley Museum and Library.)

After coming from the cow, milk was tested and cooled to 40 degrees in ice; only then could it be bottled. In the early days, milk came from the barns in sealed cans that moved from one building to another via a system of pulleys. These dairymaids are using a primitive device, which was simply a vat on casters, to bottle and seal by hand. (Courtesy Hagley Museum and Library.)

By the mid-1920s, when George Kearney (left) and Bill Doran (right) posed by a Milwaukee D automatic rotary filler, mechanization made a big difference in the bottling process. In one minute, workers could fill and cap 38 quarts or 58 pints of milk. Some plants with high-speed machines could process 5,000 bottles an hour. (Courtesy Hagley Museum and Library.)

In 1903, the Pennsylvania Railroad opened a station at 32nd and Market Streets in West Philadelphia. George Wood, who served on the railroad's board, built his milk depot housing an office and distribution center across the street at 32nd Street and Woodland Avenue. Designed by the same architect who did the milk house in Wawa, the Philadelphia building featured ornamentation, such as the keystones above the windows, which appeared on a new dairy erected in 1929. Milk arrived by train from Wawa and went to the ice-filled refrigeration room before being loaded on milk wagons for delivery in less than 12 hours since from coming from the cow. These wagons, seen on the streets six days out of seven, were like rolling advertisements for the dairy and the deliverymen its ambassadors. (Courtesy Hagley Museum and Library.)

"Wawa" for us!

At the beginning of the 20th century, babies and children were the target market for certified milk, and these healthy tykes posed for a 1905 dairy brochure that claimed "man cannot improve Nature's product so all we do is keep it clean" and cool.

Some dairies used horses and wagons for home delivery in Philadelphia into the 1940s, but not Wawa. The company purchased its first autocar in 1914. Manufactured in Ardmore, Pennsylvania, it had a two-cylinder engine that produced 20 horsepower and operated at a top speed of 17 miles per hour. It is pictured in front of the West Philadelphia milk depot. (Courtesy Hagley Museum and Library.)

In winter, Wawa cows lived in clean, well-ventilated stables, but in summer they spent their days in pastures like this one at a farm called "the Willows." Twice a day they were brought into the milking barn where 1910 USDA rules prohibited the presence of "dogs, cats, or loafers." Generally, the quantity of milk produced per cow was greater during grazing months of the year. (Courtesy Hagley Museum and Library.)

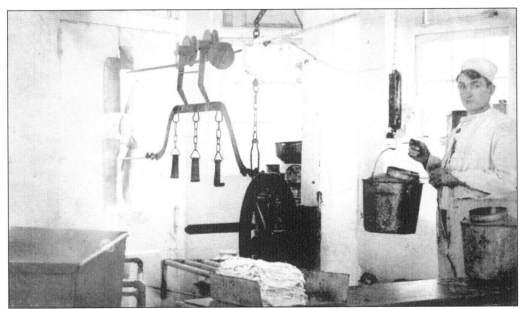

Each milking barn had a special area for weighing milk. Full pails arrived on lines operated by a system of pulleys and were lifted onto a spring balance suspended in a convenient position. The weight of the pail was subtracted and the remainder entered in the milk register as the quantity yielded by a cow. Average yields per day were 10 quarts or 25–26 pounds. (Courtesy Hagley Museum and Library.)

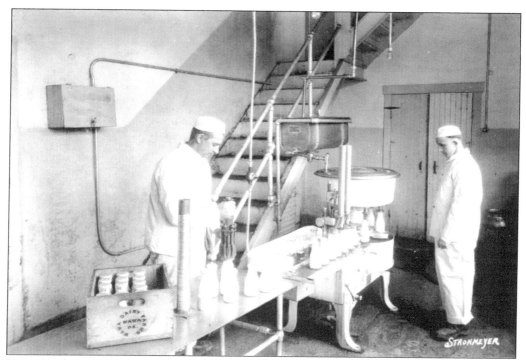

H. A. Strohmeyer Jr., a well-known New York photographer of animals, visited Wawa with the Eastern Guernsey Breeder's Association in 1926, taking a series of photographs inside the dairy. This one shows a rotary filler and bottle capper. Capping involved three steps: applying an inner plug cap, an outer crinkly hood, and a wire sealer. (Courtesy Hagley Museum and Library.)

In 1913, the U. S. Patent Office recognized the central cloverleaf design and double outer ring as a registered trademark. George Wood's 1909 application noted use of the trademark, without words, on milk, cream, butter, and cottage cheese labels since January 1, 1904.

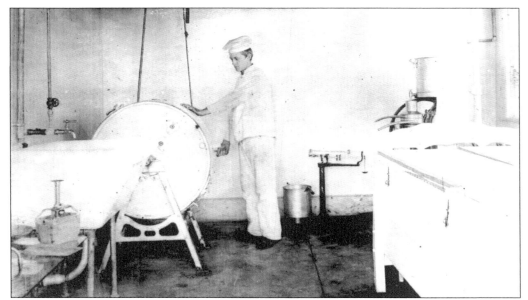

Butter making is a simpler process than cheese making, but still requires know-how to avoid being greasy. This photograph shows a worker operating a churn. There is a butter mold in the left foreground, and the top of a de Laval separator is visible on the right. At Wawa, butter was produced as a by-product, with the skim milk being made into cottage cheese. (Courtesy Hagley Museum and Library.)

USDA rule No. 24 for working with cows stated, "The milker should wear a clean outer garment, used only when milking and kept in a clean place at other times." These men began their day at lockers containing their clean white uniforms, which were laundered at Wawa. Some caps do not have visors because the milkers laid their heads against the cow's side during milking. (Courtesy Hagley Museum and Library.)

Harry Farber, manager of the dairy from 1910 to 1948, began working at Wawa in 1907 and recalled there were no cars anywhere in the vicinity at that time. He oversaw the transition of milk processing from the 1902 milk house to a new plant built in 1929. Described as "dapper but informal" by a Wawa veterinarian, he was outdone in the clothes department by the chief herdsman Charles Rife, who "dressed as if going to a board meeting at a bank." Rife managed the cow production program for the certified and pasteurized herds. Both men were committed to excellence and delivering high-quality dairy products that satisfied and delighted customers. They had the respect of their employees and enjoyed a cordial relationship, which was important since they, and many of their workers, lived in houses on dairy property. (Courtesy Hagley Museum and Library.)

Early in the 20th century, urban milk markets began grading milk, but there was no universal standard. That changed in 1910 with the creation of a milk standards commission and the familiar letter grades. In 1914, dairies serving Philadelphia agreed to voluntary grading, and 10 years later the Grade A Pasteurized Milk Ordinance took effect. The National Dairy Council promoted milk as a "necessary food for growth and health," urging the use of more dairy products and declaring ice cream "not a luxury, nor merely a holiday tid-bit [but] a delicious, refreshing, stimulating, nourishing food" that was available at the local drugstore. That is where this advertisement for Grade A Wawa milk turned up during a building renovation in Paoli, on Philadelphia's Main Line. The image of the beauty with the bobbed hair and pearls sipping a glass of Wawa milk reminded customers that the high-quality product delivered to their doorsteps was also available for fountain treats like ice cream, sodas, and milk shakes.

Five

FROM FARM TO STORE

Through the 1920s, Wawa increased its share of Philadelphia's fresh milk market by offering milk and cream of the highest quality, but the 1902 dairy could no longer support demand. In addition, local health boards expanded requirements for producing certified milk. By 1928, regulations called for separate plants to process certified and pasteurized products. Projected costs were staggering. Fortunately, the McCormick Company of Pittsburgh and New York worked out a creative solution through ingenious engineering and designed two plants in one building. Construction began in 1928, and the dairy opened a year later. (Courtesy Hagley Museum and Library.)

When the new plant opened, only certified cows remained on the adjoining farm. Milk for pasteurization came from herds on other Wawa farms and by purchase from neighboring farms. This view of the main pasteurizing department, taken from the visitor's observation room, shows hygienic white tile walls and the gravity flow arrangement of processing from the milk heating equipment at the top through the holding and cooling system in the middle to the bottle fillers below. Sterilized bottles full of Primrose milk moved along ribbon conveyors to a separate casing area. A corridor, described by the health department as a barrier, ran outside all the certified rooms so that workers passed through this inner lock when moving from one room to another. All ceilings in this department were arched to prevent condensation, and features like steel window sashes and hospital operating room lighting fixtures exceeded the rigid requirements for bottling certified milk. A unique arrangement allowed for the conservation of resources and used steam generated by pasteurization to sterilize certified bottles. (Courtesy Hagley Museum and Library.)

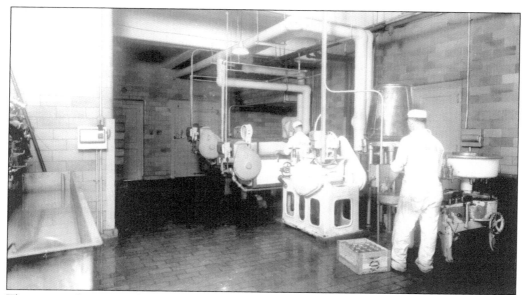

The principal purpose of a dairy is the processing of fluid milk, which also produces skim milk, whey, and various types of cream. These can be put to good use to make other dairy products. Wawa enjoyed a fine reputation for quality buttermilk, cottage cheese, butter, and creams, all made from pasteurized milk in the by-products room on the second floor of the new plant. (Courtesy Hagley Museum and Library.)

The shipping platform, water tower, rear view of upper levels of the pasteurization department, and part of the power plant are visible in this 1929 photograph taken as part of a series documenting the exterior and interior of the new, ultramodern $250,000 processing plant. Some of these photographs illustrate an article on the dairy in *Milk Plant Monthly*, June 1933. (Courtesy Hagley Museum and Library.)

When George Wood started his dairy, he built the milk house on a farm lane well away from the main road that bordered his property. In contrast, the brick 1929 plant, with its full height four-column Classical-style portico, sits squarely along U.S. Route 1 and is boldly identified as Wawa Dairy Farms. The building itself reflects the dramatic growth of the business in the 1920s, and Wawa's continued commitment to supplying customers with a wide selection of high-quality certified and pasteurized milk products. Because the main office and distribution center were located in Philadelphia, the new plant contained only a general office area, laboratory, and reception counter for greeting visitors and making retail sales. Plant manager Harry Farber waited on a customer contemplating a purchase of Wawa butter, packaged in a carton like the one seen on the facing page. Many more halfpints of milk were distributed over this counter to groups of schoolchildren, Cub Scouts, student nurses, and others who toured the plant. (Courtesy Hagley Museum and Library.)

Plants set up solely to produce butter are called creameries. As a dairy, Wawa's main product is fluid milk and butter was a by-product. Just as there are grades of milk, there are different types of cream based on butterfat content. Cream used to make butter contains 40 percent butterfat. This sample carton and the accompanying door hanger (below) are the first known use of a Canada goose on Wawa's packaging.

Until the 1950s, the milkman and his delivery truck were the principal form of dairy advertising. Drivers were encouraged to leave sample bottles of milk at doors of potential customers. This door hanger shows an oversize Canada goose above the new plant and a bottle proclaiming the benefits of certified milk. The cloverleaf trademark, in use since 1904, was adapted to serve both the Clover Sweet and Primrose product lines.

In 1929, the same year the new dairy plant opened, Wawa changed the location of the main office and distribution center in Philadelphia, moving to the north side of Allegheny Avenue east of 35th Street, not far from where U.S. Route 1 crossed the Schuylkill River. By this time, milk no longer moved by train into the city, and the new facility was conveniently situated for delivery by truck. In addition to an office and refrigerator room, the building had ample room for truck storage and maintenance. About the time this photograph was made in 1934, Wawa served 48 retail home delivery routes from Allegheny Avenue. But the dairy, like the individuals it served, struggled through the Depression, mortgaging nearly all its property for $500,000 in 1932. Small advertisements, with slogans such as "Buy health by the bottle," appeared in modest giveaway booklets distributed by the Lucky Lady Shopping Guide Company in 1933. This outreach built upon good will generated by donations of milk, cream, and butter to school bazaars, church and synagogue socials, and relief efforts.

The dairy business grew, declined, boomed, and leveled off during the period of the mid-1930s through the 1940s as cataclysmic world events affected lives everywhere. Wawa made due, purchasing new trucks as needed (above) and selling the herd in 1945. Despite this fundamental change, the dairy complex looked much the same (below). World War II gasoline rationing had an impact on home delivery that was offset by a brisk wholesale business. Each day 30,000 pints of Wawa milk made their way to the Philadelphia Navy Yard, where many empty bottles were thrown overboard and others were stowed away as reminders of home. In April 1943, the dairy president received a letter from a member of the Royal Navy enclosing a Clover Sweet bottle cap found aboard an invasion craft that saw duty in North Africa. (Courtesy Hagley Museum and Library.)

Wearing a white coverall and cap similar to those worn years before, Pete McLean (above) is inspecting bottles in 1949 as they move from the Milwaukee filler. Machines used earlier in processing are pictured below in a photograph from the early 1950s. The worker is monitoring a pasteurizer, a cylindrical tank with an agitator in which the milk was heated to 145 degrees for 30 minutes before being pumped out and cooled to 36 degrees. This method is known as batch pasteurization and is no longer used. Now the process is called HTST, for high temperature (165 degrees) and short time (16 seconds). The large white machine in the foreground is a homogenizer that reduced the size of fat globules in the milk so they would stay in suspension, eliminating the cream layer. (Courtesy Hagley Museum and Library.)

Why GOLDEN GUERNSEY

Presented by

Wawa Dairy Farms

that Special Milk GOLDEN GUERNSEY *A National Habit*

After the war, the nonprofit Golden Guernsey Association stepped up efforts to proclaim the merits of milk consumption in general and Golden Guernsey milk in particular. Claiming "milk is not just milk," the brochure urged homemakers to have their families sleep with the windows open, "work hard, play hard and smile." Of course, the perfect fuel for this ideal life was Golden Guernsey milk. The rich yellow color was due to the presence of the carotene in Vitamin A, other vitamins and minerals, and a high butterfat content of 4.5–5 percent, which made for a distinctive cream line. One quart provided 40 percent of an adult's daily protein needs. Beyond eye appeal, nutritional value, and the milk's reputed fine flavor, Golden Guernsey had the equivalent of celebrity endorsement because athletes used it when training, and Guernsey cows accompanied Admiral Byrd on his expedition to the South Pole.

Wawa milkman Tom Summers, seen here in 1955, epitomized the home delivery salesman of the 1950s. He was a veteran of World War II and was drawn to the work because he liked the schedule of five weeks on and one week off, as well as the independence and responsibility of keeping track of accounts, collecting money, and turning it in. This entrepreneurial spirit was bolstered by raffles and promotions designed to attract new customers and introduce existing customers to additional dairy products. Milkmen were frequently entrusted with keys to a customer's house, and on occasion, they performed truly heroic feats. Driver Frank Verna received the Pasteur Award as an outstanding humanitarian for rescuing a family of three small children from a burning building. Verna, Summers, and their fellow milkmen drove the streets of Philadelphia and its suburbs to deliver quality dairy products in a timely manner, but often the service and trust that accompanied the milk enriched the exchange for both customer and milkman.

The dairy undertook a series of mergers and purchases in the 1950s in an attempt to consolidate routes and expand retail home delivery business. Brookmead Dairy, purchased in 1950, had eight routes on Philadelphia's Main Line, giving Wawa an increased share of that market. Wawa was already a presence in Chester when it purchased Crystle Dairy, but the largest acquisition came in 1958 with the purchase of Turner-Westcott. A new logo appeared on home delivery trucks (above), on the sides of buses, and on a billboard atop the 69th Street Terminal in Upper Darby. The snub hood Divco trucks had the clutch and brake in one piece and were driven standing up, a challenge offset by the low-slung body that made it easy for the driver to get in and out. (Below, courtesy Hagley Museum and Library.)

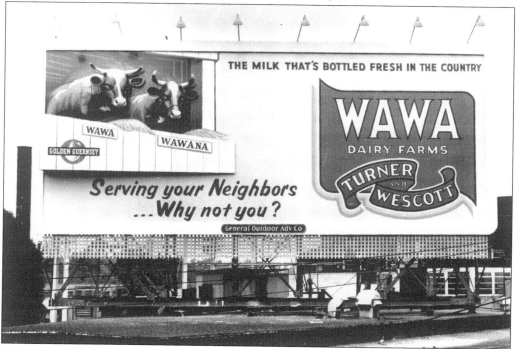

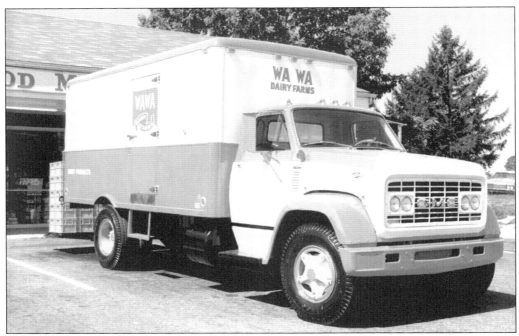

As early as 1922, there were reports of the infant supermarket industry's attempts to capture a share of the milk trade. These markets continued to erode the home delivery business, but the impact was not felt until after World War II. At Wawa, sales declined from 1959 through 1962, reflecting a trend away from home delivery because of rising costs, changing patterns of milk consumption, and grocery shopping via automobile. It became obvious that one deliveryman could serve a few wholesale customers in less time than it took several drivers to complete home delivery retail routes. In 1963, Grahame Wood proposed entering the convenience store business "because company owned and operated stores are captive customers." Dairy wholesale trucks served the first stores but were soon replaced by a fleet of tractor trailers (below). (Above, courtesy Hagley Museum and Library.)

Veteran employee Ethel Tyers, now retired, was born on Alfalfa Lane when it was home to the families of farm and dairy workers. In 1976, she was the only woman working in the dairy plant. This 1992 photograph shows Ethel at the half-gallon filler monitoring sealing and date stamping of paper cartons of milk. (Martin Kane photograph, courtesy Hagley Museum and Library.)

In the 1990s, for several years in a row, Wawa won the prestigious product excellence award given by Master Dairies, a nationwide association of large, independent dairies. Wawa products were judged in a yearlong competition against 25 of the largest independent dairies in the United States. (Martin Kane photograph, courtesy Hagley Museum and Library.)

Wawa's <u>Fresh</u> Heavy Cream

Preferred by Famous Philadelphia Chefs.

CREAM OF THE CREAM — Georges Perrier (l.) of "Le Bec-Fin" and Marcel Brousette (r.) of "La Camargue" demand Wawa's heavy cream for their menus. The two restaurateurs think Al Leifl (c.), Wawa Dairies' "milkman," delivers the freshest, most flavorful cream in town. You might not want to drink it by the glass — it's almost 40% butterfat — but you can't find a better cream for soups, pastries, and anything else you make in your famous kitchen.

Ask our manager for this product.

Wawa dairy serves over 900 wholesale customers. These include famous restaurants, neighborhood eateries, airlines, hospitals, and schools. Each wholesale customer requires different products in an array of sizes from tiny creamers to gallons. Continued improvements in processing, packaging, and delivery keep Wawa poised to meet the needs of the wholesale market while satisfying individual customers.

Three barns on the dairy property became warehouses for produce, tobacco, and candy products when Wawa entered the convenience store business in 1964. A refrigerated cooler adjoining the dairy served as a warehouse for delicatessen meats, cheeses, and other perishables. In 1976, a new tobacco and candy (T & C) warehouse opened, followed by a new perishables warehouse in 1983. A multilevel addition to T & C in 1992 modernized the facility. For several decades, the warehouse complex maintained and supplied more than half the products carried by Wawa stores. (Martin Kane photographs, courtesy Hagley Museum and Library.)

Valley Road was once a farm lane running in front of the 1902 dairy. It was paved and a bridge over Rocky Run was constructed under a 1930s WPA project. Afterwards, the road divided dairy property, leaving houses on Alfalfa Lane and another residence on one side and the dairy complex on the other. In 1994, Wawa proposed a land development plan to modernize its buildings, increase production capability, and safely integrate the property. Called DWD, for the dairy, warehouse, and distribution operations, the expansion involved moving tons of earth and leveling outmoded barns and farm outbuildings. Construction projects included a state-of-the-art fleet maintenance facility, office building with a conference center, and new refrigerated warehouse and loading facility. The 1929 dairy plant was enlarged and renovated with care to preserve its architectural significance. Completed in 2001, these projects and the accompanying landscaping transformed the property, but what brought improvements on both sides of Valley Road together was a new vehicular bridge, dedicated on December 6, 1999, as Wild Goose Crossing.

Changing trends in the beverage industry led to increased demand for noncarbonated drinks. Wawa responded by expanding the offering of iced teas, flavored teas, and fruit juices. Since 1997, juices and teas are bottled in clear PET (polyethylene terephthalate) containers with twist-off caps. Convenient packaging and a full line of beverages resulted in increased sales with the dairy producing more juices and teas than milk in the peak summer months.

One goal of effective warehouse management is picking orders safely with speed and accuracy. Wawa's high-tech Automated Storage and Retrieval System (AS/RS) is a sophisticated computerized system featuring 16 double-sided aisles that store 80,000 cases at a time and move them at a speed of one per second. Operated from a control room, the AS/RS sorts refrigerated products by type and destination, organizing the crates for efficient loading and delivery.

100 years fresh!

WAWA DAIRY · 1902 · 100 YEARS · 2002

Wawa Vitamins A&D Added 1% Milkfat Grade A · Lowfat Milk

Wawa Vitamin D Grade A Milk

Wawa Vitamins A&D Added 1% Milkfat Grade A · Lowfat Chocolate Milk

Wawa
My choice, my Wawa!

©2002 Wawa, Inc.

At the beginning of the last century, George Wood built a dairy to bottle fresh milk products from certified Guernsey cows. He added a city milk depot and bought trucks to ensure timely delivery of a highly perishable product. Milk from Wawa Dairy Farms received accolades from physicians and consumers who requested Wawa products even on vacation. Satisfied customers spread the word. Wawa responded to increased demand, changing preferences and dairy industry regulations by expanding the product line to include pasteurized milk products. An ultramodern dairy in a Classical-style brick building that was actually two processing plants in one signaled Wawa's continued commitment to delivering perishable products of the highest quality. That 70-year-old plant looks the same on the outside but houses high-tech computerized systems for processing and packaging juices, teas, and other beverages in addition to milk products. Over 100 years ago, Wawa introduced the Clover Sweet brand. Now, Wawa brand noncarbonated beverages continue traditions of quality and freshness. Ongoing expansion and renovation position Wawa Dairy to become the largest noncarbonated beverage center on the East Coast.

Six

WAWA FOOD MARKETS

On April 16, 1964, in Folsom, Pennsylvania, Wawa opened its first convenience store. Consumer shopping patterns changed, and convenience stores provided an easy shopping alternative. The first Wawa was so successful that, in 1964, two others were built and the $50,000 loan to build all three stores was quickly repaid. This happened because of a new leader at Wawa: Grahame Wood, grandson of George Wood. He reinvented the company with a commitment to delight customers.

Grahame Wood (1915–1982) began his career at his grandfather's company, George Wood, Sons & Company, selling cotton products produced at the family's Millville Manufacturing Company. He also served on the board of Wawa Dairy Farms and grappled with the decline of both businesses. Synthetic fibers and changing tastes eroded the cotton business. Shifts in patterns of milk consumption combined with the growing popularity of supermarket shopping reduced demand for home delivery of milk. Wood, a graduate of the University of Pennsylvania and veteran of service as a paratrooper in World War II, recognized a challenge when he saw one. He knew the textile business was a lost cause, but the dairy could be saved and just needed an outlet for its products. The idea of a convenience store selling Wawa milk and other merchandise was born. He visited King Kwik convenience stores in Ohio, a chain operated by friends, and came home with a plan that persuaded the board of directors to enter retail food marketing. Today's business reflects his vision, tenacity, and leadership. (Courtesy Hagley Museum and Library.)

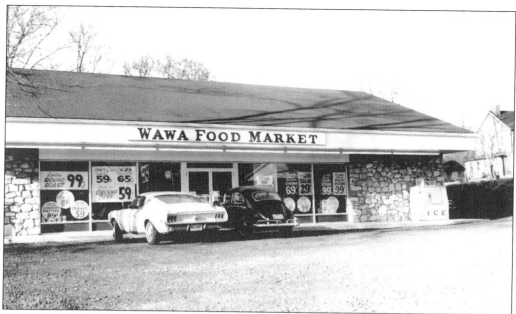

This is a typical Wawa store. It is modest, but for the customer in 1964, the Wawa stores were a wonderful shopping experience. Grahame Wood insisted that, before the Wawa name went on any store, it was to be clean and staffed with friendly, attentive people. The prices were fair. The stores were stocked with fresh foods like delicatessen meats, vegetables, fruits, dairy products, and groceries. In 1964, Wawa was one of the only places where, after 6 p.m. or on Sundays, you could buy fresh products. Although perishables were challenging to handle, Grahame believed they kept customers coming back. (Courtesy Hagley Museum and Library.)

In October 1968, Wawa stores expanded to New Jersey. The company opened its 36th store in Millville on land once owned by the Millville Manufacturing Company. Mayor Bill Shaw and city officials attended the opening of the store, located at Sharp and Columbia Avenues. Within a decade, Millville and neighboring Vineland had a total of 12 stores serving their neighborhoods.

WAWA KITCHENS
fried chicken | fish & chips

HAMBURGERS 20c

Welcome to our colorful Wawa Kitchens where you can now get delicious, hurry-up lunches, dinners and snacks. Either eat here or take home in our special "Take Home" packages which help retain that piping hot flavor.

Grahame Wood knew that success had no finish line, and this belief kept the company experimenting. Wawa opened more than 50 stores by 1970, while continuing to try new things, adapt, and listen to the customer. This included attempts at food service, including Wawa Kitchens. Most of these ideas failed in the early days, but they set the stage for the innovations that years later reinvented Wawa.

These were humble beginnings. The first headquarters for the food store chain was in an old tenant house located on the Wawa Dairy property. It did not have air conditioning or the conveniences of a modern office. However, the little white house on the hill was filled with enthusiasm. Very soon, explosive company growth required that the operations move to a bigger building.

Wawa Chain's Growth Matches Consumers' Changing Tastes

WAWA, PA. — Changing consumer tastes and buying patterns gave birth to Wawa Food Markets, a 41-unit chain of convenience stores headquartered here.

Back in 1963, the retail operation was just a gleam in the eye of Grahame Wood, founder and chief executive officer of the convenience store chain.

Wawa Dairy Farms, in business before the turn of the century, was faced with declining sales of home-delivered milk. With the growth of the suburban shopping centers, housewives were flocking to the supermarkets and making their milk purchases while attending to their other food needs.

As an experiment, Mr. Wood decided to open retail stores — primarily as an outlet for Wawa Dairy's products. Shopper response was enthusiastic and the stores quickly evolved into full-line convenience operations.

But Grahame Wood and his col-

HEADQUARTERS: Chain headquarters, including central buying offices and training center, are housed in this charming country home. When not working, employes can use nearby swimming pool and tennis

Fortunately, the perfect building became available. It was Red Roof, once the home of George Wood. Not only was it nearby and spacious, but it provided a link to the heritage and values. The lovely gardens and grounds were used for company meetings and picnics.

73

Connecticut residents had no idea this was a convenience store with a difference. Newspaper articles reported, "The name puzzles most people," but that curiosity drew them to store openings. Seen here on August 12, 1971, at opening ceremonies in West Haven, Connecticut, are, from left to right, Grahame Wood, Adam Bozzuto, and Lester Broadbelt.

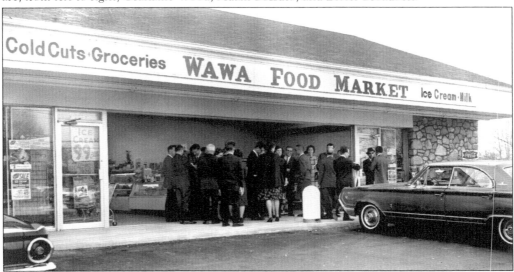

It is business education day and teachers come to learn all about Wawa. (Courtesy Hagley Museum and Library.)

Expansion boomed, and in 1972, Wawa opened its 100th store in Marlton, New Jersey. In this photograph taken at the grand opening, Miss New Jersey, Gail Hackerman, greets customers. By the end of the year, Wawa had 130 stores in five states—Pennsylvania, New Jersey, Delaware, Maryland, and Connecticut. (Courtesy Hagley Museum and Library.)

Wawa kept innovating. In February 1972, Tom Laudenslager (holding the gallon jug), vice president of Wawa Dairies, and Lester Broadbelt, president of Wawa Food Markets, discuss plans with Hercules Corporation executives for the manufacture and sale of Wawa bottled water. It failed, as did many other ideas such as self-serve laundries, hydroponic tomatoes, Wawa horseradish, Wawa cigars, and rug shampoo machine rentals. Nevertheless, Wawa learned from its mistakes and kept innovating.

In the 1970s, Wawa opened 24-hour stores. Customers were working and playing around the clock. The stores were known as friendly beacons of light and became a regular shopping place for workers on night shift, police on patrol, and firefighters. Wawa was there for its community morning, noon, and night. In 1971, supermarkets opened on Sundays, extended hours during the week, and added air conditioning and service delis. They became more convenient. As a result of the increased competition, Grahame Wood realized Wawa must adapt and innovate forever.

When you're in a hurry...and you've got to shop fast, stop in a Wawa Market. We're a grocery store, delicatessen, dairy and general store...all in one modern market. Our quick self-service and hi-speed check out guarantee you the World's Fastest Shopping Trip!

Customers are in a hurry. "People on the go" was more than a slogan for Wawa; it became the company's mantra. To fulfill it, Wawa sought store sites with more parking, added more convenience products, eliminated displays to reduce clutter, and repositioned key items, such as newspapers, to the front of the store. In addition, the search criteria for new store locations considered traffic patterns equally or more important than the number of nearby homes.

In the 1970s, the checkout area was designed for efficiency rather than customer convenience, which often led to lines. There are no lines for this young customer, but he is not stuck behind someone ordering deli products, which seemed to take forever. That changed with a new store design that separated the two areas. (Courtesy Hagley Museum and Library.)

To increase the speed of service, Wawa separated the deli from the checkout area. All stores were remodeled to include the innovative design, and staffing levels increased to include a minimum of two people on duty at all times. Wawa made a huge commitment to give customers more convenience.

During a break in the filming of a Wawa commercial, Vic Musso, store manager, shares some laughs with legendary Philadelphia Eagles middle linebacker Bill Bergey. In the commercial, Bergey emphasizes the speed of service that he enjoys when shopping at Wawa. Bergey's line: "I sure do love linebacking on the football field, but I hate long lines at the supermarket . . . so when I'm on the run, I always stop at Wawa."

Grahame Wood identified his successor, second cousin Richard D. Wood Jr., a young Philadelphia lawyer. The first thing Dick did was work in the stores because he recognized the importance of listening to customers and associates. Dick continued this and the practice of store tours through the years. He considered the people on the front line to be critical to the company's success.

In 1975, the Delaware County Chamber of Commerce honored Wawa for remarkable growth and ability to adapt to consumers' changing tastes. In this photograph, Grahame Wood accepts the award. He is shown with Lester Broadbelt (left), president of Wawa Food Markets, and Samuel Parsons of the chamber of commerce. In 1977, Dick Wood became president in anticipation of Grahame and Lester's retirement. Grahame died in 1982. His influence, however, serves as an inspiration today. Those who knew him remember his grace, humility, and entrepreneurial spirit. (Courtesy Hagley Museum and Library.)

Seven

TRANSFORMING THE STORES

How did Wawa manage to transform itself from a small chain of food markets into a way of life, into something customers refer to affectionately as "My Wawa?" A new generation of leadership began to focus on solutions to further simplify customers' daily lives, while providing a personal connection—something that distinguishes Wawa from other retailers. In the period from the late 1970s to the mid-1990s, Wawa made dramatic transitions, reflected in the changing design of these coffee cups. (Duane Perry photograph.)

These are Wawa groupies. They are at the Wawa every day because they say they cannot get through the day without the wit, wisdom, and smiles of the folks at their Wawa. In 1980, Wawa began selling its own blend of coffee, formulated to the taste of customers in the Delaware Valley (the area roughly within a 100-mile radius of Philadelphia). In a few years, Wawa coffee became legendary. Wawa stores became the meeting place both for customers on the go and for neighbors.

Capt. Eric Guenther Jr. (left) and 1st Lt. Lawrence Field enjoy Wawa coffee in Bosnia. The 1st Troop Philadelphia City Cavalry was mobilized for task force Noble Eagle stationed at Camp Morgan, and they requested that Wawa ship coffee to their troop. The coffee was a real morale booster because the smell and taste were reminders of home.

The origin of Wawa coffee is traced to the mid-1970s to a few stores where enterprising store managers responded to requests from customers for freshly brewed coffee along with their morning paper. Every year, sales of coffee increased. By the late 1980s, Wawa coffee had become the company's most profitable product. Today, the famous coffee brand keeps customers coming back every day.

When customers requested that Wawa managers make hoagies, managers responded because delighting customers is a tradition at Wawa. However, hoagie customers are known for being picky about how their hoagie should be made. Yet it is these passionately particular customers who became Wawa's next opportunity.

To win their trust, stores were designed so that hoagies were built right before customers' eyes. Associates were trained to make the famous sandwich any way the customer wanted. Within a few years, Wawa became the No. 1 retailer of hoagies in the Delaware Valley.

Wawa has a hoagie size to suit every appetite—the Classic, the Shorti, and the Junior. Soon, the Shorti became the No. 1 selling hoagie, and the Junior was a favorite among many customers who wanted a smaller sandwich. The line continues to expand and now includes a vegetarian variety of this traditional favorite. By the mid-1980s, dietitians recommended Wawa as a place where customers on the go could get a variety of delicious choices, such as fresh fruits, soups, yogurts, and of course, their favorite hoagie.

By the late 1980s, Dick Wood had identified the principles that have guided the company through both turbulent and terrific times. Some examples include practicing leadership by celebration; no executive dining rooms; making good long-term decisions even if they lead to painful short-term consequences; striving to be the best, not the biggest; and being vigilant to the needs of the customers. Dick also acknowledged, "Our informal environment could drive others nuts." And he firmly believed it was his job to create an environment where each associate could make a difference. He demonstrated his commitment to these principles and values by staying in close touch with associates and customers through store tours and town meetings. He also participated in dozens of charitable and community activities. (Bill Johnson photograph.)

Too busy to cook? Today anything that takes more than 12 minutes to cook is considered inconvenient. More and more Americans eat out and people living alone find cooking burdensome. At the same time, people are beginning to tire of fast food. Is this an opportunity for Wawa to put sit-down restaurants in the stores? Wawa tried some of these, but they did not catch on. As a result, Wawa refocused on its core business—takeout products for people on the go.

In the 1970s and 1980s, the major oil companies added mini-marts to their gas stations. Wawa's first attempts to sell gasoline were low-key. The stores were limited in space and had just a few pumps, no canopy, and prices on the high side. It was the right idea, but the wrong execution. In the mid-1980s, gasoline operations were shut down at Wawa.

In the mid-1990s, Wawa tried gasoline again. This time Wawa did it right. Dick Wood led the effort, studied the industry, and oversaw the development of the system for buying gasoline. The new stores were larger and featured public restrooms. Dick even headed up the committee to ensure that they remain spotless.

By 1980, Wawa had several stores along the New Jersey coast. Despite the conventional wisdom that says doing business will be difficult, Wawa was interested in expanding at the shore. From seasonal sales to staffing difficulties, Wawa proved it could swim upstream successfully. The challenge turned into an opportunity.

By the end of the 1980s, Wawa had opened over 50 stores along the New Jersey shore, its most successful expansion during the decade. The company met staffing challenges with an international recruiting program. These three Irish lasses are part of the international connection, a solution that helps keep Wawa stores staffed through Labor Day as European colleges resume in October.

By the early 1990s, customers demanded value from every food retailer. Fast food chains offered deal meals. Wawa featured many products such as 12 packs of soda at highly competitive prices. Wawa coupled these with featured takeout foods. One of the most popular was the two-foot hoagie, an exclusive innovation from Wawa packaged in a redesigned box similar to those used by florists for long-stemmed roses.

No surcharge, no sir. At the same time that every other retailer charged customers to use the ATM, Wawa offered the service with no surcharge. This is another example of how Wawa adds value to the shopping experience.

By the early 1990s, Wawa had developed a strong loyalty for coffee and hoagies. Yet, attempts to develop hot food-service products were mediocre. All the company had to show for it were hot dogs, meatballs, and hot plates to heat soup. Wawa knew it was time to try something more professional for hot foods.

Wawa introduced national brands such as Taco Bell in 75 stores. Customers liked getting the products at Wawa, but it was not profitable enough to sustain labor, so the project failed. Nevertheless, Wawa managers learned food-service systems and procedures that proved valuable in the future. Also, the customers asked Wawa to build its own brands.

In 1994, bigger stores helped Wawa continue to meet customers' needs. Wawa opened two huge stores—4,780 square feet, each with a roster calling for as many as a dozen associates to be on duty at one time. Wawa learned it had to build a bolder and bigger store, with room for new systems, new equipment, and more customers. The stores had 50 or more parking places.

It is December 1994 at the grand opening celebration of the new Wawa store in Tinicum, Pennsylvania. Wawa associates are shown dressed up to welcome the neighborhood to the new, big Wawa. From day one, customers loved it. The complexity of the business is challenging, but Wawa people are committed to make it work for the customers.

Inside, the stores sparkled and featured a wide variety of freshly prepared foods and specialty coffees. Food retailing executives from around the world visited two stores to view Wawa's innovative concepts. The stores were featured in industry publications and presentations.

"They said it couldn't be done." The conventional wisdom was that a convenience store works because it is a simple business, but Wawa introduced new products and services that made the business complex, so it was back-to-school for many Wawa associates. Every associate commits to lifelong learning, innovation, and adaptation on the job, in school and in technology. They learn more than how to manage a complex store. They learn how to build the future.

The team pictured above is called the Clockers because they measure everything Wawa does. They are part of Wawa's operations engineering team, and they develop processes to make the store work smoother and easier for customers and associates. The key to success is having people on the team who have experience in the real world. Teams at Wawa, like the one pictured below, use a total quality system for managing projects. The system is a variation on the methods pioneered by W. Edwards Deming, but with more focus on customer satisfaction. (Above, Duane Perry photograph.)

Over 1,000 store managers and suppliers attended the Wawa Conference and circus-themed trade show in 1997. The biennial event demonstrates the company's commitment to innovation, adaptation, and the continuous learning needed to align and involve store managers with business plans. It is also an opportunity for managers to swap stories and have fun.

Retail is a demanding business, so one of Wawa's rules is to have fun. Therefore, it is only appropriate that at the store manager conference the management committee dresses up to entertain store managers. CEO Dick Wood calls it humanization through self-humiliation. (Duane Perry photograph.)

Wawa's new prototype stores, like the one above in Chadds Ford, Pennsylvania, demonstrate dramatic changes in store design and product offering. The stores are large and built on two to three acres with anywhere from 50 to 100 parking spaces on attractively landscaped, well-lit lots. The gasoline offer is state-of-the-art with 12 to 20 fueling positions, credit acceptance at

the pump, and environmental technology that is among the best in the industry. Inside, the store features 7,600 square feet of space, and an interior design that showcases our brands and our people. In 2004, over 140 of Wawa's 540 stores sold gasoline. (Joe Mullan photograph.)

Offering full-service gasoline around-the-clock come rain or shine is a huge effort. New Jersey is one of only two states that do not allow self-service gasoline. In New Jersey, conventional wisdom is that it is too difficult for retailers to run a full-service, high-volume gasoline operation. Wawa meets the challenge and currently operates 35 stores with full-service gas in New Jersey. (Duane Perry photograph.)

Eight

MORE THAN A STORE

Wawa is passionate about its customers. The Wawa brand of convenience, quality, and personal connection appeals to a diverse group of customers, from busy moms and students to construction workers and executives. Many of them depend on Wawa to simplify their lives. Wawa recognizes that it must continue to adapt by understanding customers' needs and offering quality products in stores staffed by friendly, attentive associates.

"What is Wawa and what is the brand?" asks Howard Stoeckel, chief operating officer of Wawa. The Wawa brand is unique because of the stores and products but, most of all, because of the people. He dons the duds of the brand ranger and tours the company spreading this message to all 15,000 associates: "It begins with the basics, and it begins with you. You are the brand."

High standards make the Wawa brand unique. More than a million customers come through the doors every day. It is a challenge to keep things sparkling, but the associates do it. It takes a team working together like clockwork, and they do it. It takes enthusiasm, and they have it.

Store manager Flo Palazza and an associate review the Wawa Brand Standards (WBS) checklist. The measurement system is directly linked to customer satisfaction, and it focuses on safety, sanitation, in-stock conditions, and product quality. Wawa Brand Standards exemplify Wawa's promise to customers and associates.

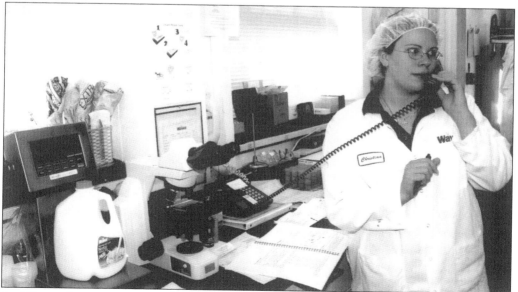

At Wawa, the experience working with perishables and the commitment for sanitary food handling began over a century ago when George Wood started the Wawa Dairy. That heritage lives on today. Wawa quality experts assure that the products are fresh, safe, and delicious every step of the way, from farm to dairy to store.

"Want a fresh pot of coffee?" says Charlie. "No problem." That means brewing fresh coffee constantly and dumping old coffee every 20 minutes. Known as Mr. Wawa Coffee by customers, Charlie was a Wawa coffee host until he died in 2002. He started working for Wawa in 1961 as a driver for the dairy. The attention to detail provided by coffee hosts like Charlie makes a great brand and a great cup of coffee.

The Wawa brand requires world-class facilities—not too big so they remain convenient, but not too small because they require expanded space in the food service area for ovens and other equipment necessary for food preparation and storage.

Hoagies went high-tech with the installation of customer activated terminals (CAT) in all Wawa stores. This cutting-edge technology allows customers to order sandwiches, hoagies, and food service items through a touch screen terminal. The initiative simplifies the ordering process by increasing accuracy and speed of service.

We eat with our eyes. Wawa's bakery case gives the customer a feast from the very first glance. Wawa is about attractive store design. Customers say that the layout and spice colors of the interior make them feel at home.

My choice, My Wawa. From the beginning, Wawa stores offered variety in dairy and fresh products, something unavailable at most other convenience outlets. The Wawa brand continues to be about choice, and the company is always innovating to maintain high-quality standards while offering a variety of products.

It's 4 p.m. What's for dinner? Wawa to the rescue with soups, wraps, sandwiches, hoagies, breaded chicken, and Hot To Go Bowls. All are made from fresh ingredients in a wide variety of choices.

It is time to toss the hats and cheer. In 1996, Wawa opened its first Virginia store. Even before groundbreaking, Wawa hired full-time associates. During construction, the associates participate in community and charitable activities. "It's a way that we get to know the people in the community, let them know what our values are and have some fun as a team," said area manager Jim Shortall.

In new markets, family nights, held before stores open, are a way of helping new associates understand the culture and tradition that makes Wawa unique. Wawa managers invite associates and their families to a fun evening of prizes, music, and celebration.

Antoinette Essa from WWST-TV reported from Virginia's second Hoagie Day event in July 2002, when a hoagie of heroic proportions (1,776 feet), built by Wawa associates, was served to the local community. The event recognized heroes from area emergency services. Teams from the U.S. Army and Marines competed in a friendly hoagie-building competition and earned funds for area charities.

By 2004, the majority of Wawa's over 540 stores were located within a 100-mile radius of Philadelphia. Three are larger experimental stores of over 7,000 square feet. Manager Ed Sanchez welcomes customers to his store in Chadds Ford, Pennsylvania. "It's an oasis in my frazzled routine," says a customer who relies on Wawa brands to simplify her life.

Who owns Wawa? The majority of company stock is owned by over 130 descendants of George Wood. Company associates who participate in the Employee Stock Ownership Plan (ESOP) have over a 25 percent ownership stake. The bond between the Wood family and the associates is fundamental to Wawa's core values and success. Every year, Wood family members gather at Wawa headquarters to learn about the business and share kinship.

Wawa is a culture that values open communication, and annual shareholders' meetings are one way of sharing information. Here, shareholders and ESOP participants gather for a meal following the meeting.

Celebration is not just a tradition. It is a heartfelt way to say, "We are family." At a service awards ceremony in 1980, Grahame and Dick Wood congratulate Karen Owsley. Karen joined the company in 1978 and is currently a computer graphics and archives specialist. Like many Wawa associates, Karen has other family members who work for the company.

At the grand reopening of the Wawa in Aberdeen, Maryland, customers and the community show support for the store team and celebrate the rebuilt and expanded store. Whenever the stores are closed for a remodel, the customers are reminded how much they miss their store and the associates.

It is opening day for the new store in the Fox Chase section of Philadelphia. It was the first Wawa in Philadelphia to have both the convenience store and gasoline, something that customers here have been requesting. It is a big job to find a site like this and build the store, so on opening day there were plenty of reasons to cheer. Wawa uses celebrations to thank associates as well as the community.

110

The Philadelphia City Hall was the backdrop for Wawa Hoagie Day 2001. Designed by John McArthur Jr., the building occupies one full city block. The hoagie served at the event was 10,000 feet long, weighed 4½ tons, and completely surrounded the country's largest municipal building.

Frequent Wawa customers often develop relationships with a particular store and its team—the "My Wawa" phenomenon. "Besides great coffee, I come here for the entertainment. It's a daily celebration I wouldn't miss," says Ken MacDonald Sr., a customer pictured here with store associates Mary Anne Cunningham and Doreen Sheehan.

Dave Fletcher, pictured here with Dick Wood, and 32 store managers received the Golden Wings Award in March 2000. Managers select the recipients of Wawa's most coveted award. Dave and the other winners are role models who exemplify Wawa's values.

Over nearly four decades, Paul Modugno drove nearly four million miles through rain, blizzards, hurricanes, and blistering heat with no accidents. Thère du Pont, vice president, presents him with a crystal trophy to honor the amazing safety record. Thère also championed a program to make Wawa one of the most safety-conscious retailers in America.

Olé! The President's Club is a time to celebrate Wawa's best. Cancun, the jewel of the Mexican Caribbean, is a past location for Wawa's President's Club. Each year, Wawa recognizes store managers who displayed an unparalleled commitment to excellence. The highlight of the President's Club is the ring ceremony. The President's Club ring is the symbol of their success.

Val Connery is the only Wawa store manager to be inducted into the President's Club every year since the program's inception. Before she received her 14th President's Club award, Val entered the stadium on horseback showered by roses from her peers.

The three-night getaway features celebratory events like lobster dinners on the beach and offers a chance for President's Club inductees to share the myriad experiences and challenges of being a store manager who strives to live Wawa's values.

A perfect score means prizes, music, and fun for the entire store team. Each month, the Wawa Prize Patrol hits the road to create an instant celebration in stores that achieve exceptional scores for safety, cleanliness, friendly service, and fresh products.

Manager Tony Davis and his store team receive the coveted brand standards trophy. Stores that consistently win enjoy dinners, trips, and other celebrations. Some associates get trips to Disney World. One part-time associate and her spouse won a trip around the world.

Dancing in the aisles encourages customers to join in a prize patrol celebration to acknowledge the store associates for the things they do every day to make their lives a little brighter.

In order to demonstrate how local government and business can work together, Pennsylvania governor Ed Rendell loaned his name to a limited-time wrap sandwich at Wawa. The Rendelli wrap recipe was created based on the governor's well-known love of chicken wings. He and Wawa agreed upon the idea to benefit an educational charity.

In August 1990, Wawa associates march in a parade for America's birthday party in Philadelphia. Earlier that day, Wawa served cake and ice cream to thousands, including freedom medal recipient, president Jimmy Carter. Celebrating freedom is a tradition for Philadelphia, and Wawa is very much a part of the city's culture.

At Wawa's 10th Hoagie Day (in 2001), it took only 17 minutes for the mile-long hoagie to disappear. Over 13,000 people enjoyed Philadelphia's official sandwich. The day included an outrageous hoagie-eating contest and guest appearances by past and present Philadelphia mayors Ed Rendell and John Street. Hoagie Day is always a fabulous salute to the community.

Wawa associates share a passion for winning, so Hoagie Day is a whole lot more than balloons and hoopla. It is a big job that takes Wawa's own unique teamwork. The same teamwork is needed every day to successfully serve lunch rush crowds.

Another Wawa signature celebration is the Finest versus Bravest contest pitting local police officers against local firefighters to determine who can build the most hoagies in five minutes. Both teams win money for their favorite charities.

Wawa celebrates an exceptional associate, Ariel Shiner. He is an Eden Institute participant. The Eden Institute is a nonprofit organization dedicated to research and help for people with autism and their families. Ari began work in 1981 at the Wawa store in Princeton, New Jersey. He has worked there for over two decades. The recognition is made by Joe Bendas, who hired Ari and coached him along the way.

Wawa CEO Dick Wood applauds Daniel, a participant of the Wawa house, during the ribbon-cutting ceremony. This facility is a key part of the Eden Institute's pioneering program to provide early diagnosis and intervention for infants and toddlers with autism.

Wawa has a long history of partnering with the American Red Cross and NBC 10 to raise funds for disaster victims. In 1993, over $100,000 was raised to help victims of Hurricane Andrew. After the tragic events of September 11, 2001, Wawa customers contributed $1.8 million to the American Red Cross Disaster Relief Fund. In every community at every Wawa, neighbors waste no time giving to others who need their help.

Wawa has a tradition of supporting Children's Hospital of Philadelphia. At the Children's Miracle Network telethon in 1996, Wawa associates present a check for over $100,000 representing the proceeds of an in-store fundraising campaign. In addition to fundraising, Wawa associates volunteer at Children's Hospital, and Dick Wood serves on its board.

During Take Kids to Work Day at Wawa, Tommy Fitzpatrick tells children all about driving an 18-wheeler. Children participate in activities throughout the day that give them insights into Wawa's culture and the working lives of their parents.

Jim Shortall and his daughter participate in the Walk for Juvenile Diabetes. Hundreds of Wawa associates and their family members raise funds for diabetes research, SIDS, the Race for the Cure, and other worthwhile charities. Sometimes associates champion a charity because of personal experience. All of them do it because they want to make a difference.

In September 2003, Hurricane Isabel hit the East Coast. The most damage was in Virginia. During Isabel, Wawa associates worked day and night to keep stores open to serve the community in times of crisis. In emergencies like these, Wawa stores are deemed essential to the communities.

At a 2003 Wawa awards ceremony in the Bahamas, Chrissy Callahan (bottom row, center) poses with managers from her area. A year before, Chrissy had been diagnosed with cancer. She was concerned she would be unable to manage her store during her medical treatment, but Chrissy's team did so well for her, she was selected among Wawa's best managers and invited to attend the President's Club. Wawa employees support each other through tough times.

Fran Cardillo (left) and Edward Guarino (right) drop by Store No. 1 in Folsom, Pennsylvania, to check progress on the remodel. It is the fourth major remodel since the store was opened. Forty years ago, they watched the store being built. "We've been coming here every day since then. We see our friends and we start our day with a smile."

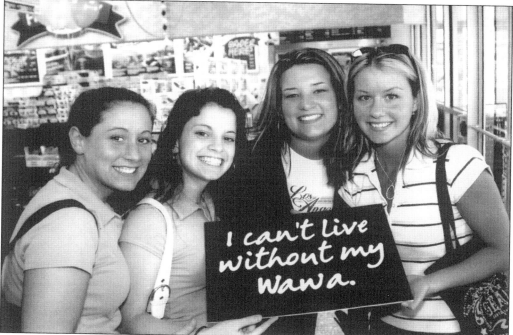

On April 16, 2004, in Folsom, Pennsylvania, the grand reopening and 40th anniversary celebration filled the store with friends and neighbors. Like these four girls, they echo the phrase "I can't live without my Wawa!"

Kristin Smith attended the Folsom store reopening. When she moved to the area, she was amazed at the devotion of customers to their Wawa. Kristin joined the staff of the *Delaware County Daily Times* and wrote not one, but two major articles to explain the phenomenon. The headline is taken from a line so often heard, "Wawa is more than a store, it's a way of life."

One customer said, "When things get hectic, it is a joy to stop by Wawa. They have what I need. They make me feel at home. It's an island of calm in this crazy world."

Dozens of customers packed the store during a birthday bash for Grandmom Pat Sacco. She is pictured here with store manager Lori Cavanagh. Grandmom Pat is 89 years old and works almost every day because she thinks of the customers as part of her family. "Every day—rain, shine, or snow up to your waist—they drive miles to be here, so I'm not going to disappoint them. And about the celebration, it's nice. However, the best celebration is the one that happens every day between people who care about each other."

Many customers think of Wawa as more than a store thanks to the enthusiasm and commitment of the thousands of associates who work in the stores. In fact, the hundreds of associates behind the scenes, from the mailroom to the computer room, from real estate managers to financial specialists and other teams throughout Red Roof, DWD and regional offices are equally as committed to the customer experience through support of store teams. Visitors to Wawa's headquarters say they feel the enthusiasm from the moment they are greeted by the smiling receptionist, Kathleen Monte.